Aliens

Jim Pipe

WAYLAND

First published in 2011 by Wayland

Wayland
Hachette Children's Books
338 Euston Road
London NW1 3BH

Wayland Australia
Level 17/207 Kent Street,
Sydney, NSW 2000

Editor: Paul Manning
Designer: Paul Manning
Proof-reader/indexer: Alice Harman

Produced for Wayland by
White-Thomson Publishing Ltd

www.wtpub.co.uk
+44 (0)845 362 8240

Pipe, Jim, 1966-
Aliens. -- (Twilight realm)
1. Human-alien encounters--Juvenile literature.
2. Life on other planets--Juvenile literature.
I. Title II. Series
001.9'42-dc22

ISBN 9780 7502 6661 1

Printed in China

Wayland is a division of Hachette Children's Books
an Hachette UK company
www.hachette.co.uk

Picture Credits
t=top **b**=bottom
13t, 15b,16b, 18t, 19 (H.G. Wells and Orson Welles),
21: Wikimedia Commons. All other images © Shutterstock and Dreamstime.

Contents

We Are Not Alone...

In many sightings, aliens are described as small, grey creatures with black, glassy eyes.

Scientists have long believed that there may be alien life out there somewhere. But have aliens from outer space ever visited Earth? Where do they come from and what do they look like?

Over the past 60 years, there have been thousands of reports of mysterious flying saucers hovering overhead, or bright lights shooting across the night sky. Dozens of people also claim to have met aliens. Some stories are clearly hoaxes, like the 'Venusians' met by George Adamski in the California desert in 1953 (we now know that conditions on Venus make it impossible for intelligent life to exist there). But other reports are harder to explain away – like the puzzling 'nests' of flattened reeds that Australian farmer George Pedley said were made by an alien spacecraft in 1966. Unidentified Flying Objects, or UFOs, *do* exist. But are they alien craft, top-secret test planes or bizarre tricks of the light caused by freak weather conditions?

The Quest for ET

Ever since human beings first gazed into the night sky, people have dreamed of discovering life on other planets. But it was not until 1971 that scientists were able to begin listening for radio signals from deep space.

Somewhere out in the vastness of the cosmos, there is every chance that extraterrestrials (ETs) do exist. But it's unlikely we'll get to meet them. The nearest star to our Sun, Proxima Centauri, would take our fastest spacecraft about 70,000 years to reach!

But do we really *want* to meet ET? Suppose that aliens came to wipe us out and take over our planet? Even if they were friendly, they might bring with them diseases that would be deadly for human beings.

▼ *A great place to start looking for intelligent life is on planets outside our solar system. So far, some 540 such planets have been found, many by instruments like this roaming coronograph used in NASA's Kepler mission.*

'I imagine they might exist in massive ships, having used up all the resources from their home planet. Such advanced aliens would perhaps become nomads, looking to conquer and colonize whatever planets they can reach.'

Scientist Stephen Hawking on aliens

UFO Alert!

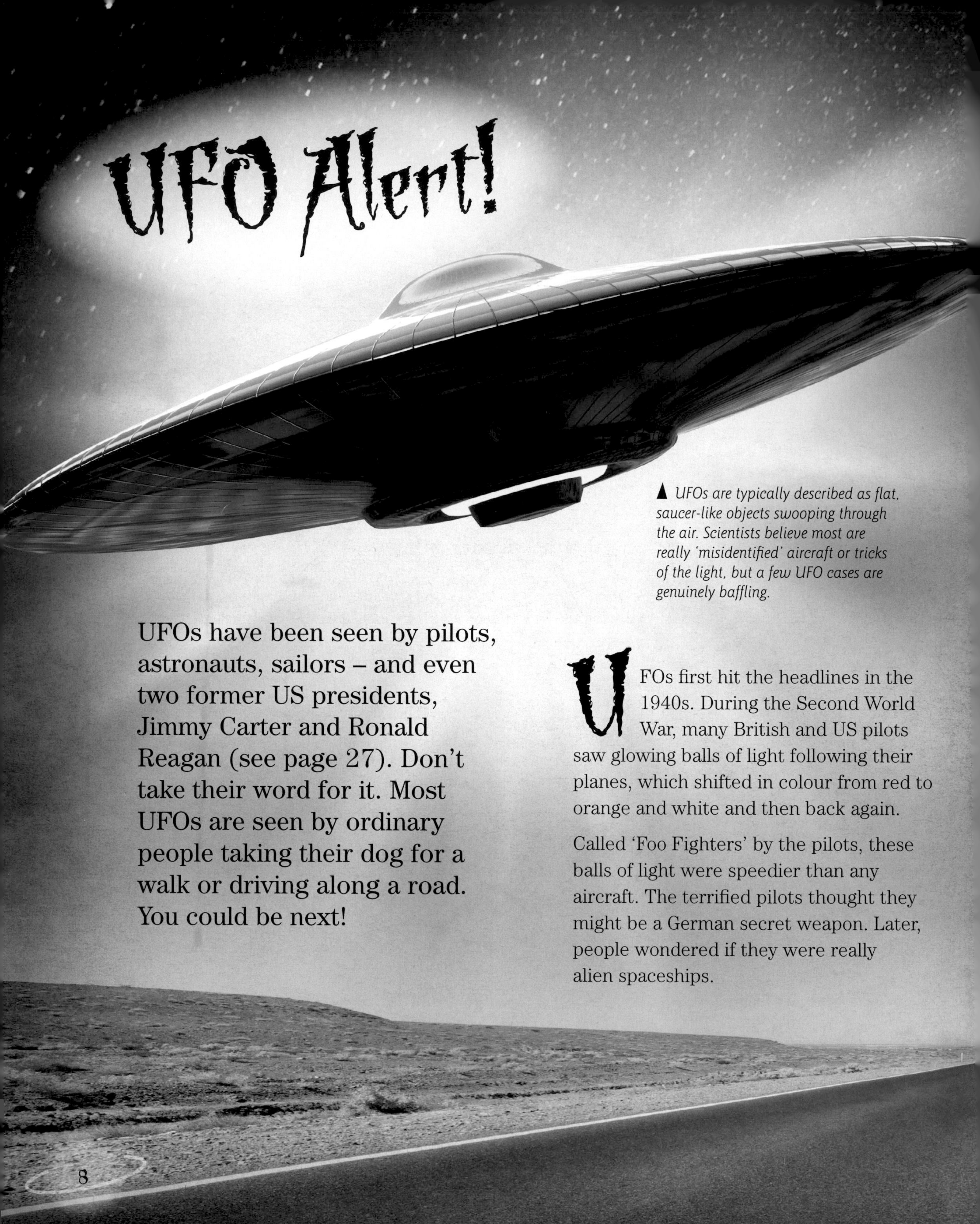

▲ *UFOs are typically described as flat, saucer-like objects swooping through the air. Scientists believe most are really 'misidentified' aircraft or tricks of the light, but a few UFO cases are genuinely baffling.*

UFOs have been seen by pilots, astronauts, sailors – and even two former US presidents, Jimmy Carter and Ronald Reagan (see page 27). Don't take their word for it. Most UFOs are seen by ordinary people taking their dog for a walk or driving along a road. You could be next!

UFOs first hit the headlines in the 1940s. During the Second World War, many British and US pilots saw glowing balls of light following their planes, which shifted in colour from red to orange and white and then back again.

Called 'Foo Fighters' by the pilots, these balls of light were speedier than any aircraft. The terrified pilots thought they might be a German secret weapon. Later, people wondered if they were really alien spaceships.

By the 1950s, flying saucers were a major news story. Many were seen with the naked eye, but in 1956, a radar station in Bentwaters, Norfolk, UK, tracked a UFO moving at over 15,000 km/h! In 1976, a jet fighter spotted a UFO over the city of Tehran, Iran, and was about to open fire when its weapons suddenly refused to function. Reports still come in every year of spooky lights in the sky performing aerobatic feats that would be impossible for normal planes.

Yes, most UFOs can be explained away as passing aircraft, satellites, balloons, or strangely-shaped clouds. But some 5 per cent remain a mystery. Many are picked up on radar and spotted by trained observers such as pilots, police and military personnel. Often the evidence is compelling. Even so, it's hard to prove if these UFOs really are piloted by visiting aliens.

'UFO' is a modern term, but people have been spotting weird objects in the sky for centuries. In 1088, a Chinese scholar wrote about a huge flying object that was able to take off at tremendous speed and cast a blinding light for ten miles around!

The First 'Flying Saucer'

On 24 June 1947, US pilot Kenneth Arnold was flying a small plane near Mount Rainier, Washington, when he saw a bright flash in the sky. Looking closer, he claims he saw nine V-shaped UFOs travelling at speeds of over 1,600 km/h. Arnold later described how the fleet of alien craft flew across a mountain crest like saucers skimming over water.

Arnold's sighting was soon headline news all over the world. Within months, there were hundreds of similar reports of 'flying saucers' across America.

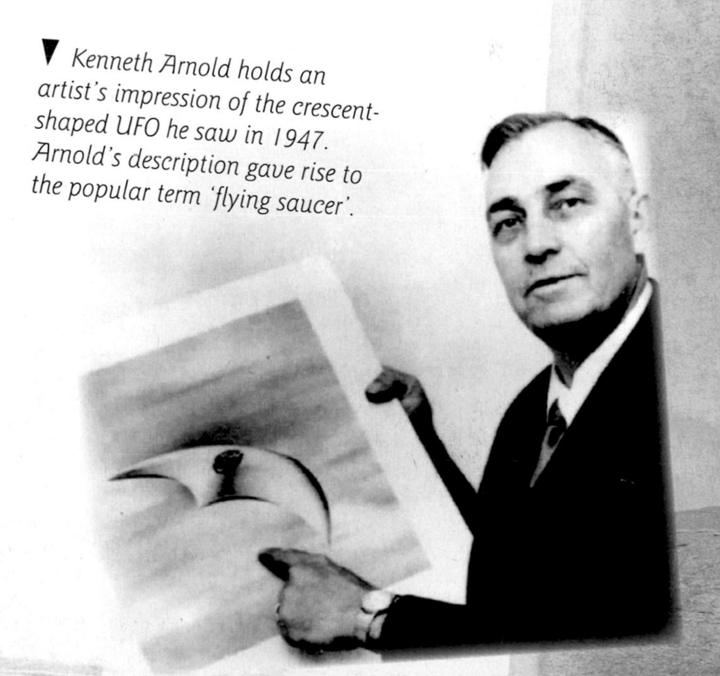

▼ *Kenneth Arnold holds an artist's impression of the crescent-shaped UFO he saw in 1947. Arnold's description gave rise to the popular term 'flying saucer'.*

Close Encounters

▼ *This giant tower of rock in Wyoming, USA, is the scene of an epic meeting between humans and aliens in the1977 Steven Spielberg film,* Close Encounters of the Third Kind.

Imagine driving down a lonely country road at night. Suddenly you're blinded by a dazzling light. The massive bulk of an alien craft blocks the road ahead. Shadowy alien figures emerge and surround you. What do you do? How do you describe your experience to other people?

The term 'close encounter' first appeared in the 1970s, when the American UFO expert Dr Allen J. Hynek came up with a new way of describing alien sightings.

In Hynek's new jargon, the type of sighting that took place in Lubbock, Texas, USA, in 1951, when local people reported mysterious lights whizzing over their town in a 'V' formation, was a 'close encounter of the first kind' ('CE1'). In the second type, a 'CE2', some physical trace is left behind after the sighting – such as tracks on the ground or flattened crops. When aliens are spotted, it's a 'CE3' – as in the tale of policeman Lonnie Zamora.

In April 1964, Zamora was driving along a road in New Mexico, USA, when he claims he saw a silvery object on four legs. Spooked by Zamora's car, two small figures nearby hopped into the spacecraft. It immediately took off with a mighty roar, leaving behind patches of scorched earth.

Attack of the Goblins

UFO sightings can be frightening enough, but imagine encountering aliens face to face!

On 21 August 1955, Kentucky farmer Billy Ray Taylor and his wife were visiting their friend 'Lucky' Sutton, when Taylor claims he saw a 'large shining disc' land nearby. When he ran to tell the Suttons, they laughed at him. But after Sutton's dog began barking, both men went to investigate – and reportedly saw a hideous goblin-like creature heading towards them.

Terrified, the men ran back inside. Soon, other creatures were swarming over the roof and peering in through the windows. Shooting at them had no effect. After several hours under siege, the Sutton and Taylor families fled in two cars to the local police station. Though investigators looked for evidence, no trace of the landing or the aliens was ever found.

'It was a serious thing to him. … It was fresh in his mind until the day he died. He never cracked a smile when he told the story…. He got pale and you could see it in his eyes. He was scared to death.'

'Lucky' Sutton's daughter, Geraldine Hawkins

▲ *The alien 'goblins' seen at the Sutton farm were said to have upright pointed ears, flat noses, thin limbs and claw-like hands.*

Alien Abduction

Tales of people being kidnapped by aliens are not as rare as you might think. Often they are dramatic, detailed – and freaky!

On 5 November 1975, 18-year-old logger Travis Walton was heading home from work in the forests of Arizona, USA, when he and his workmates saw what they described as a large glowing disc hovering above a clearing. When Walton walked closer, he claims that a blue-green ray from the craft blasted him backwards. Thinking him dead, his friends fled the scene. When they returned later, Walton had vanished.

Five days later, Walton turned up in a nearby town, claiming to have been abducted by aliens. Two doctors examined him, but found nothing unusual. At the spot where Walton had been zapped by the 'ray', police found no signs of burning. Yet, under hypnosis, Walton gave detailed, vivid descriptions of his alien captors and their spacecraft. He still stands by his story today.

► *Dazzling lights, strange sounds, terrifying sensations – but is the nightmare of alien abduction real or imagined?*

An Alien Starchart?

In September 1961, US couple Betty and Barney Hill were driving home through New Hampshire, USA, when they reported seeing a giant UFO ahead. It loomed closer until it floated right above them. They felt a tingling sensation – then everything went blank.

When they awoke the next morning, they found curious marks on their bodies and a strange pink powder on Betty's dress. They also realized they had 'lost' two hours.

Days later, Betty began to have troubled dreams in which she met aliens on board a spacecraft. The aliens appeared as human-like figures just over 1.5 metres tall, with greyish skins and 'wrap-around' eyes.

Betty drew a chart, which she claims the aliens had shown her on the spaceship. It showed a star system in another part of the galaxy. Incredibly, this group of stars, Zeta Reticuli, was not discovered by astronomers until eight years later!

▲ *After her reported alien encounter, Betty described having nightmares in which aliens carried out medical tests on her. They cut off a lock of her hair, saved trimmings from her fingernails and tried to pull out one of her teeth.*

Could YOU have been kidnapped by aliens without knowing it? Check the symptoms below. All have been reported by claimed victims of alien abduction:

- Nightmares about aliens
- Puzzling illnesses, such as headaches, feeling sick or being unable to sleep
- 'Missing time', when you can't remember where you've been for whole periods at a stretch
- Unexplained scars or bruises
- Feeling of having flown through the air without knowing why or how
- Strange black marks that show up on an X-ray of your body
- Memories of flashing lights or being covered in liquid.

▲ *Forced medical examinations are a common theme in abduction stories. In 1957, Brazilian farmer Antonio Villas Boas claimed he was snatched by aliens, stripped and covered in a strange jelly before being forced to give blood.*

Watching the Skies

Why not try a spot of UFO hunting yourself? Make a regular skywatch from a hill or open space. Write down as many details as you can, and try to take a photo of any unusual objects flying overhead. Be warned, aliens aren't fussy about where they land!

UFOs aren't called 'phantoms of the night' for nothing. It can be very hard to prove a genuine sighting. Often pictures of UFOs are fuzzy, or the saucer appears too far off to be identified with any certainty – so it helps to take friends along who can confirm what you've seen.

Do watch carefully – planes, meteors and old satellites falling through the sky can easily be mistaken for flying saucers. So can the planets Venus or Jupiter shining brightly in the night sky.

If you do get lucky and a UFO appears nearby, remember to run away from it as fast as you can. You wouldn't want to be abducted by aliens...

▼ *Nighttime UFOs are called 'nocturnal lights' while daytime UFOs are called 'daylight discs'. Whenever you head out, be sure to take the right gadgets with you. Here are some suggestions:*

UFO-WATCHING CHECKLIST

- Pen and paper for making notes
- Video camera
- Telescope
- Binoculars
- Star charts
- Maps
- Mobile phone
- Device for speedy Internet research
- Infra-red thermal-imaging equipment for very dark nights
- Night vision goggles

UFOs: Where to Look

Researchers have noticed that UFO sightings tend to come in waves or 'flaps' that happen every few years. Often these occur in particular places, lasting anything from a few days to a couple of weeks.

- There have been more UFO sightings in Brazil than any other country in the world.
- The supposed alien crash landing near Roswell, New Mexico, USA, is just one of many mysterious events reported in the notorious 'Texas Triangle'.
- The Nullarbor Plain, a vast treeless desert in southwestern Australia, is a focus of intense UFO activity.
- A remote area near the Ural mountains in Russia is known as the 'M-triangle'. Locals here have reported everything from strange lights and signs written in the sky to glowing aliens in the forest.

If you do see a UFO, you're in good company:

'It was big, it was very bright, it changed colours and it was about the size of the moon.'

Jimmy Carter, US President, 1977–81

'I was in a plane last week when I looked out the window and saw this white light. It was zigzagging around… We followed it for several minutes.'

Ronald Reagan, US President, 1981–89

'There was something out there that, uh, was close enough to be observed and what could it be… [it] had a series of ellipses, but when you made it real sharp, it was sort of L-shaped.'

Buzz Aldrin, US astronaut

Don't just look at the sky! Strange metal objects have appeared in seas and lakes all over the world. These underwater craft are called Unidentified Submarine Objects (USOs). In 1980, over 70 people reported watching a 4.5-metre metallic object rise from the Araguari River in Brazil, hover above their heads, then shoot off into the distance.

Twilight Quiz

Could YOU join the team at MIB as a special alien investigator? Try this easy-to-answer MIB recruitment quiz!

1 You spot strange flashing lights in the sky. Should you:

- **a** Blast those pesky flying saucers out of the sky with a surface-to-air missile?
- **b** Shoot as much video footage as you can, making detailed notes on what you see?
- **c** Put your hands over your eyes and count to ten. Hopefully the lights will be gone by then.

2 A local rancher reports that one of his cattle has been horribly mutilated. Do you:

- **a** Hide yourself inside the carcass and wait to ambush the aliens when they return for another juicy beefsteak?
- **b** Take note of anything unusual, such as burn marks from landing spacecraft, unusually precise cuts or strange footprints near the carcass?
- **c** Throw up over the crime scene.

3 You're asked to interview someone who believes they've been abducted by aliens. What do you say?

- **a** 'Tell me every last gory detail. When we catch up with these guys, they're going to pay.'
- **b** 'Was anyone else there when this happened? Is there any physical evidence of what they did to you?'
- **c** 'Just write it all down on this form. That weird stuff just freaks me out.'

4 You're looking into the cold, glassy eyes of a real, live alien. What next?

- **a** Shoot first, ask questions later. ET and his friends need to realize that if they're looking for a new home, Earth is already taken.
- **b** Find a way to communicate with the alien visitor, using head and hand movements, lights or sounds.
- **c** Run through the streets, screaming that an alien invasion is on its way.

5 The MIB radio dish picks up a signal from deep space that might belong to an alien civilization. Do you:

- **a** Broadcast loud rock music back at them to scare them off?
- **b** Analyse the signal to look for patterns that might help you to understand the alien code?
- **c** Go home and start packing. If the aliens are coming, it's time to take to the hills!

CHECK YOUR SCORE

Mostly 'a's Sorry, you're too trigger-happy for this job. But if the aliens invade, we'll give you a call.

Mostly 'b's You're brave but level-headed – welcome to the team!

Mostly 'c's This job may not be for you. You'd be spooked by a flying Frisbee!

Glossary

abduction taking somebody away against their will

Aboriginal describing the earliest known inhabitants of Australia

aerobatic *(n)* describing a skilled flying manoeuvre performed for an audience on the ground

aerospace industry dealing with space flight and aviation

androids robots that look like humans

autopsy a medical examination carried out on a dead body

bacterium a tiny organism that can carry disease

chisel *(vb)* to carve wood or stone using a special tool

cinder a piece of burnt coal or wood

colonize to take over and rule the population of a country

committee a group of people who meet for a special purpose

confiscate to take away or seize

constellation a group of stars

cosmos the planets and stars that make up the universe

extraterrestrial (ET) an alien; literally, something that comes from 'outside the Earth'

firepower guns and other weapons

folklore traditional stories, beliefs and customs

furtively in a secretive or suspicious way

galaxy a network of millions or billions of stars

goblin a dwarf-like creature

gruesome horrible, revolting

harass to pester, threaten or frighten somebody

hoax a deliberate plan to trick or fool people

hybrid *(n)* something made by combining two different elements

hypnosis putting somebody into a sleepy or dreamlike state

infra-red invisible light given off by heated objects

jargon technical language that may not be understood by ordinary people

laser an intense, powerful beam of light

meteor a lump of rock or matter that flies through space

nocturnal occurring at night

nomads people who have no fixed home but travel from place to place

predator a creature that hunts others for food

puny weak or powerless

radar device for locating and tracking ships, planes or other craft

rancher *(US)* person who runs a large cattle farm

satellite a spacecraft or object which orbits the Earth

scholar a person who has made a special study of a field or subject

thermal imaging technique of photographing the heat given off by an object

tornado a type of whirlwind

ufologist a person who studies UFOs

ultraviolet a type of light found in sunlight but invisible to the human eye

undercover working in disguise or in secret

vulture large hunting bird that feeds on dead animals

x-ray special photograph that reveals organs inside the body

Further Reading and Websites

Further Reading

Aliens: An Owner's Guide, Jonathan Emmett (Macmillan Children's Books)

The Alien Hunter's Guide, Gomer Bolstrood ('Edge' series, Franklin Watts)

UFOs, David Orme ('Trailblazers' series, Ransom Publishing)

UFOs and Aliens, Anne Rooney ('Amazing Mysteries' series, Franklin Watts)

Websites

www.nuforc.org
A site where you can register your own UFO sightings.

www.top10ufo.com
A good selection of pictures and videos of UFOs.

www.ufoevidence.org
Eyewitness accounts and photographs of UFOs.

Index